ROBOT WORLD

• Robots
in Dangerous
Places

Steve Parker

W
FRANKLIN WATTS
LONDON • SYDNEY

An Appleseed Editions book

First published in 2010 by Franklin Watts
338 Euston Road, London NW1 3BH

Franklin Watts Australia
Hachette Children's Books
Level 17/207 Kent St, Sydney, NSW 2000

Created by Appleseed Editions Ltd,
Well House, Friars Hill, Guestling,
East Sussex TN35 4ET

Designed by Guy Callaby
Edited by Mary-Jane Wilkins
Picture research by Su Alexander

ISBN 978 1 4451 0039 5

Dewey Classification 629.8'92

A CIP catalogue for this book is available from
the British Library.

Picture acknowledgements
title Volker Steger/Science Photo Library; contents Peter Menzel/
Science Photo Library; 4 Mira/Alamy; 5t Hemis/Alamy, b NASA/
Carnegie Mellon University/Science Photo Library; 6 Michael
Rosenfeld/Science Faction/Corbis; 7 Niall Cotton/Alamy; 8 RJH_
RF/Alamy; 9 Hank Morgan/Science Photo Library; 10 Juniors
Bildarchiv/Alamy; 11t Peter Menzel/Science Photo Library,
b Gunter Marx/Alamy; 12 Yanns Arthus-Bertrand/Corbis;
13t Patrick Landmann/Science Photo Library, b Roger Ressmeyer/
Corbis; 14 Peter Menzel/Science Photo Library; 15t Robert Harding
Picture Library/Alamy, b Greenshoots Communications/Alamy;
16 Alexis Rosenfeld/Science Photo Library; 17 Ralph White/Corbis;
18 Michael Donne/Science Photo Library; 19t Volker Steger/
Science Photo Library, b Philippe Psaila/Science Photo Library;
20t Ballantine/Alamy, b Philippe Psaila/Science Photo Library;
21 Mike Blake/Reuters/Corbis; 22 Philippe Psaila/Science Photo
Library; 23t Hawker Siddeley Dynamics/Science Photo Library,
b US Air Force/Science Photo Library; 24 US Navy photo by Mass
Communication Specialist Seaman Apprentice Joshua Adam Nuzzo;
25t Andrew Fox/Alamy, b Richard Wareham Fotografie/Alamy;
26 Louise Murray/Science Photo Library; 27t ni press photos/Alamy,
b Francoise Demulder/Corbis; 28 Brian Snyder/Corbis; 29t Rex
Features, b Omni wheel assortment courtesy of AndyMark,Inc.
Front cover Yiorgos Karahalis/Reuters/Corbis

Printed in China

Franklin Watts is a division of Hachette
Children's Books, an Hachette UK company.
www.hachette.co.uk

Contents

Beware – danger!

Wanted: workers for **hazardous** tasks. Must be able to detect deadly fumes from volcanoes, check underground drains, measure invisible **radioactive** rays and dive to the sea bed to examine undersea pipelines. Must be fearless, reliable, obedient and hard-working. No holidays, no pay, no free time. Apply today!

Hazards everywhere

Robots are ideal workers for dangerous places. They can be made much tougher than people, with extra-strong outer casings that resist heat, cold and chemicals. They are not affected by deadly fumes or radiation. They need no air to breathe, food to eat or water to drink. They can be fitted with special equipment for their tasks, such as cameras to see in the dark, powerful grabs to hold tightly and sharp blades to cut.

◀◀ *Where there are harmful substances, chemicals or rays, people must wear specially made protective suits. Robots do not need this kind of protection.*

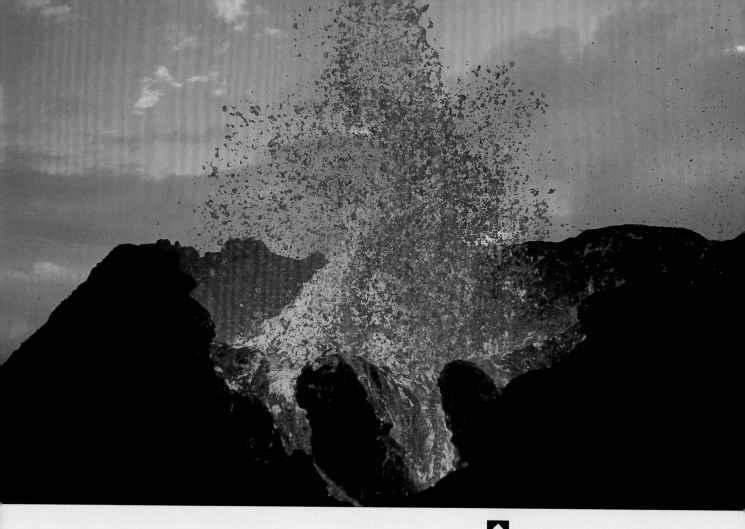

Just a machine

All round the world, robots carry out thousands of hazardous tasks daily. They check for bombs and explosive mines, and go into buildings that might collapse. They fight fires and carry out secret military missions such as spying on an enemy. Unlike people, they cannot be frightened or confused. They remain cool in the face of danger.

Some of these risk-taking robots are very clever, with a powerful computer 'brain', great strength and other amazing abilities. But they are not living beings. One great advantage of using robots is that if there's an accident, human lives are not at risk. Robots are merely machines.

Erupting volcanoes are no places for humans, but robots can withstand extreme heat, so they can collect samples of rocks and gases, and study the chemicals from which they are made.

ROBOT SUPERSTAR

Dante explores

During the 1990s the Dante series of robots crawled into Antarctic volcanoes to find out what was in volcanic gases and fumes. Dante 2 was more than three metres tall, with a spider-like shape and long legs. Wires connected it to the control base a safe distance away. Dante edged over the volcano's steep rim, ready to clamber down into the crater filled with choking fumes and hotter than an oven. Then the connecting wire broke and Dante and the scientists had to give up.

Rough and tough

Every part of a risk-taking robot is designed to cope with many hazards as well as extreme conditions. These include intense cold, great heat, falling objects, poisonous fumes and splashes of dangerous chemicals. This is why most robots designed for dangerous places have strong, wrap-around outer cases made of metal or other very tough materials.

Hot and cold

Robots are designed to cope with specific types of danger. When a person touches an object that is hotter than about 40°C, it feels uncomfortably hot. A few degrees more and human skin starts to feel pain and suffer burns. Robots can touch objects that are many times hotter – provided their engineers make them from suitable materials.

Cryogenic storage means keeping items at incredibly low temperatures. If we touched any of them, our skin and flesh would freeze solid in an instant, so robots often take over.

Hot-bots are made of **thermo-resistant** materials, which means they can withstand temperatures of several hundred degrees. These materials include certain metals, special plastics, and combined or composite materials such as GRP – glass-reinforced plastic (fibreglass plastic) and carbon fibre composite.

The importance of materials

If a robot is likely to get very hot for just a short time, then only its outer covering needs to be thermo-resistant. But if it's going to be hotter for longer, then the robot's working parts inside, such as its motors, levers and gears, also need to be able to resist heat. This gives robot engineers and materials scientists many new challenges.

Robots in very cold places are made from **cryo-resistant** materials. Some of them have small electric heaters inside, powered by their batteries, to keep their inner parts warm.

▼ *Human eyes would be permanently damaged by the intense light of this flame. A welding robot has no such problem and is not affected by the flame's heat either.*

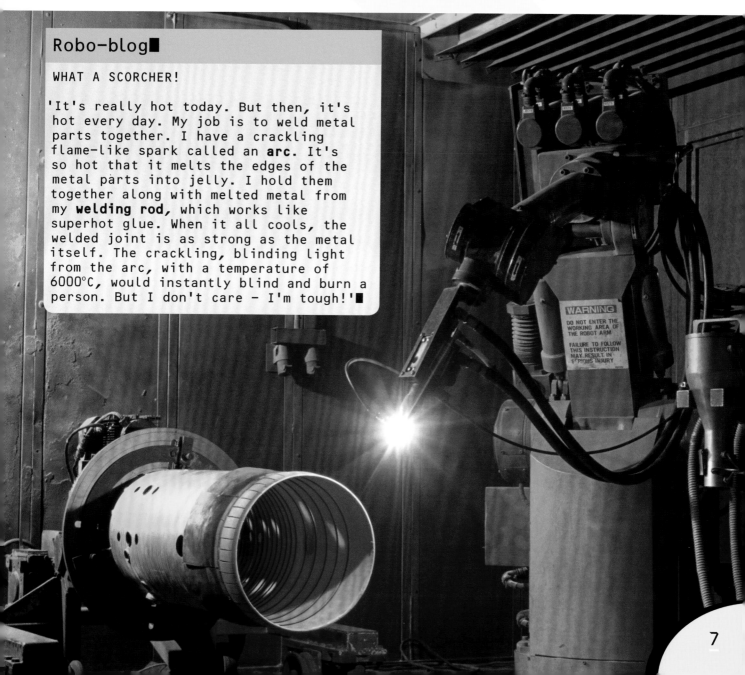

Robo-blog■

WHAT A SCORCHER!

'It's really hot today. But then, it's hot every day. My job is to weld metal parts together. I have a crackling flame-like spark called an **arc**. It's so hot that it melts the edges of the metal parts into jelly. I hold them together along with melted metal from my **welding rod**, which works like superhot glue. When it all cools, the welded joint is as strong as the metal itself. The crackling, blinding light from the arc, with a temperature of 6000°C, would instantly blind and burn a person. But I don't care – I'm tough!'■

WARNING
DO NOT ENTER THE WORKING AREA OF THE ROBOT ARM
FAILURE TO FOLLOW THIS INSTRUCTION MAY RESULT IN SERIOUS INJURY

Under control

A typical robot carries out some jobs and tasks by itself. It has moving parts such as motors, wheels, levers and gears. Robots detect what is going on around them using cameras as eyes, microphones as ears and contact **sensors** as skin. Instructions, orders or programs come from their masters – humans. Then they carry out their tasks in an automatic way... but some robots are more automatic than others.

Simple tasks

Simple robots are partly controlled by people. They do a job, for example, drilling into polar ice to see how thick it is. This is part of scientific research into **global warming** and **climate change**. The robot drillers send their results to their human controllers. Then they wait for the next instruction, about where to move and drill next.

Global warming is a huge problem. Robots can help us to study how fast it happens by measuring the temperature of the polar ocean and the ice thickness.

SnoMotes

*SnoMotes are groups or swarms of small mobile robots that travel across ice and snow to collect information about global warming. They are similar to mini-snowmobiles and they carry cameras and record temperature, ice hardness, snow depth and other measurements. Members of each swarm communicate with each other and they work out between themselves what to do next. They face daily risks such as deep **crevasses** (cracks), **avalanches** and falling through melting ice. Perhaps one day as they communicate with each other about these dangers, they might refuse to go to work!*

Clever robots

Very clever robots need almost no orders from people. These robots are called **autonomous**. This means that they can make decisions and control themselves for long periods of time. They have powerful computer brains. If they go to a dangerous place, they decide how to get there, what to do and when to escape.

Wired and wireless

Some robots are joined to a central control or base by a long cable or wire called a tether. Orders or instructions are sent as electrical signals along the wire, telling the robot what to do. Other robots are wireless – they receive and send information by radio signals. This means they are free to move around, so long as they stay within range of the radio waves. One problem with this way of communicating is that radio waves cannot travel very far through water. So underwater robots usually need tethers.

Many mobile robots have cables to bring electricity and also high-pressure oil or gas pipes to power their movements. These cables, pipes and tethers must bend and straighten perhaps millions of times without a leak or crack, and they limit where the robots can go.

Disaster scenes

Many natural disasters happen around the world: earthquakes, landslides, mudslides, **tsunamis**, cave collapses and volcanic eruptions. All of them can damage buildings, especially large buildings such as skyscrapers, schools, offices and factories. It's dangerous for human rescuers to go into damaged, weak buildings which might cave in at any moment or catch fire and fill with choking fumes. Often robots undertake rescue missions instead.

Search and rescue

Search and rescue robots, or SAR-bots, are usually quite small so they can crawl through narrow spaces in broken buildings. They have powerful electric motors and rubber caterpillar tracks to give them a strong grip as they climb over rubble or up and down stairs. They also have lights to shine in the darkness, cameras to see, and sensitive microphones to hear people calling for help. Other types of sensors include **infrared** cameras to detect the heat given off by the bodies of trapped people.

Disaster rescue teams include people, dogs to sniff and hear, equipment such as sensitive microphones to listen, and robots to explore inside broken buildings.

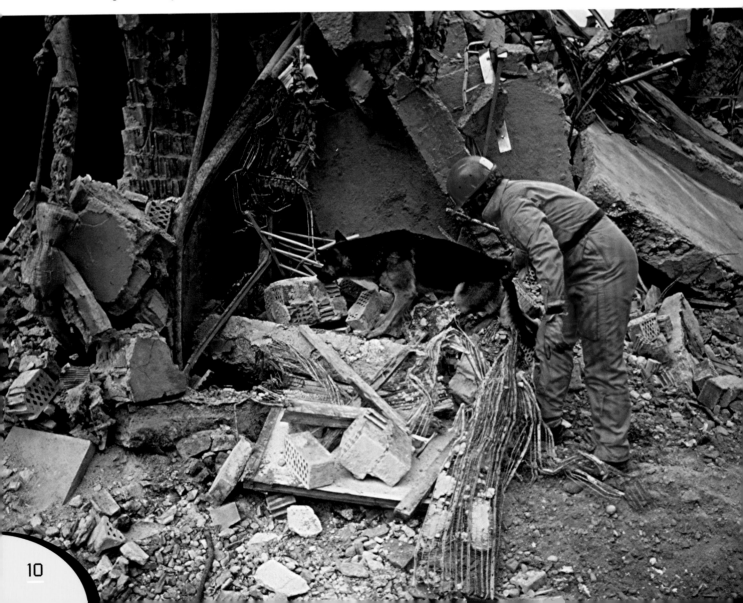

Careful control

SAR-bots are usually attached to their control centre by long cables or tethers that trail behind them as they explore in a disaster zone. Their instructions travel along the cable, along with electricity for their motors, so the robots do not need heavy batteries. Pictures and other information from the robots' sensors go back along the cable to the control centre. Here the people controlling the robot usually have someone who knows the layout of the building or site, who can guide the robot.

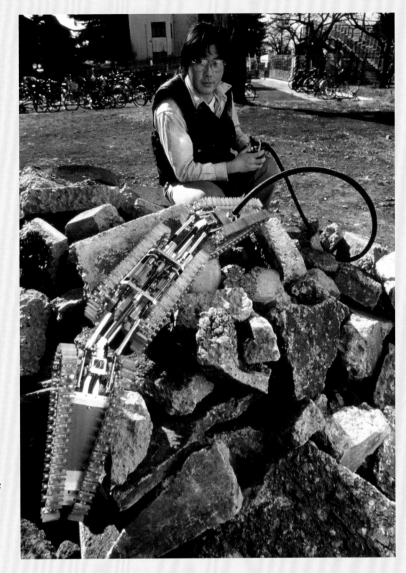

▶▶ *The Blue Dragon explorer-bot snakes its way through jumbles of rubble and small gaps, gripping with its caterpillar tracks as it searches for survivors.*

ROBO-FUTURE

Robot Paramedic

New search and rescue robots may be able to carry food, water and medicines, such as pain-killing drugs. The SAR-bot would move close to a trapped person and pass over the supplies as needed. The people at the control base can see and hear what's happening, and talk to the trapped person using a loudspeaker on the rescue robot.

▼ *If human cavers cannot fit through a narrow gap, they can send in a slim robot to take a first look at the next cavern.*

Unseen killers

Nuclear power stations make about one twelfth of all the electricity that people use around the world. The safety and security of these power stations are especially important. Nuclear accidents are rare, but when they occur they can be massive disasters. Even when a power station is running perfectly, there are areas inside where people cannot go. Enter the robots!

Dangerous rays

Nuclear power station fuel is a form of the **heavy metal uranium**. It is radioactive, which means that it gives off invisible rays and particles known as radiation. These can harm people and all living things, so it's vital to contain and control radioactivity. If any leaks or escapes, it could spread far and wide. Even on normal days, workers in a nuclear power station must be aware of radioactivity levels and keep out of high-risk areas.

▼ *In 1986 the nuclear power station at Chernobyl in the Ukraine blew up. This caused immense damage and people had to leave nearby towns such as Pripyat. Robots still help to clear the deadly radioactive material.*

▲ *Robot arms move radioactive liquids safely in a nuclear research centre. If countries generate more nuclear power in future, these types of robots will become more important.*

How robots are used

Nuclear power stations have a variety of robot-like machines such as grabs, arms and **manipulators** which work in areas with high radioactivity. The metals, plastics and other materials in the robots are not affected by the rays and particles. Some of these robots are mobile and automatic. Others are controlled by people who can see what they are doing through a glass screen that protects against radioactivity.

Toxic gases

More unseen dangers include poisonous or **toxic** gases, such as deadly **carbon monoxide** from some forms of burning, and choking **ammonia** or **chlorine** gases from chemicals. If a factory accident leaks these gases, people must leave at once. Then a robot may be sent in to find the problem and check the level of gas with its specially designed 'nose' or sniffer sensors.

ROBOT SUPERSTAR

HERO

The HERO robots were designed in the 1980s to teach people about robots and how they work, as well as being entertaining and fun. You could buy the robots ready-made, or as a kit so that you learned about the inside parts as you fitted them together. Different HERO models can sense their surroundings, move about, avoid obstacles and even talk using simple words and phrases. HERO 2000 has been programmed to pick up and deal with cans that might contain leaking radioactive material.

In the dark

Mines, tunnels and pipelines are dangerous places. Not only are they dark, they may also be full of gas, poisonous fumes, oil, chemicals and other substances. Cleaning and checking inside them is very risky for people. That's why many kinds of robots venture into the blackness.

Kurt the inspection robot checks sewers for leaks and problems. It has its own power supply and guidance system so that it comes out of the pipe network in the right place.

Pipeline pigs

Big chemical factories, **oil refineries** and industrial centres may have many kilometres of pipes and tubes to check, clean and repair. Wider, longer pipelines snake for thousands of kilometres across the land, carrying oil, gas, water and other materials. Robot machines called pipeline inspection gauges or PIGs – known as pipeline pigs – travel along inside the pipes. The pigs clean inside the pipes, remove blockages and detect breaks or leaks.

Smarter pigs

Pipeline pigs become more clever and autonomous every year. The Explorer II pig is one of the latest to inspect gas and oil pipelines. This pig moves along under its own power, instead of being pushed by the movement of the material in the pipe. It can slow down or speed up and sends out combined **electrical-magnetic waves**, which are altered by the pipe around it. The pig detects any cracks, breaks, rust or other problems in the pipe as changed patterns in the waves.

Round the bend

Explorer II's computer brain, powerful battery packs, **drive units**, sensors and other parts are enclosed in 11 linked units which are about 2.4 metres long. This design allows the robo-pig to curve round bends in the pipe like a giant string of sausages.

The Trans-Alaska Oil Pipeline is 1290 km long and has pipes 122 cm wide. Several kinds of robots regularly pass through, including scraper pigs, kink-sensing pigs and rust-detecting pigs.

Workers have to stay well away from a mine blast, but robots near the explosion can monitor it and warn of a possible collapse.

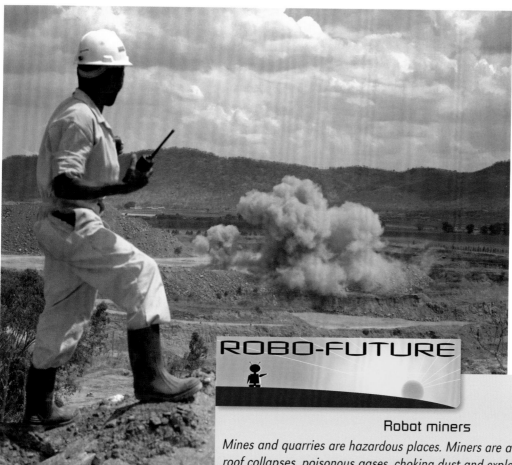

ROBO-FUTURE

Robot miners

Mines and quarries are hazardous places. Miners are at risk from rockfalls, roof collapses, poisonous gases, choking dust and explosive accidents. Robots are taking over more mining tasks. Massive robot dumper trucks trundle on programmed routes around sites. Robot roof-fixers fit panels after a tunnel is blasted or drilled, to make it safe for workers. If an area fills up with dust or sand, a robot 'mole' can burrow down to see what has happened.

Deep water

A summer paddle at the seaside is great fun. But out in the ocean there are hazards of all kinds – huge waves, strong winds, powerful tides, surging currents. Under the surface of the sea are the black depths, with intense cold and immense pressure.

Underwater rovers

For many years robots have dived deep under water. Their tasks vary from checking a ship for cracks, to observing ocean wildlife, exploring the sea bed for valuable minerals and finding treasure in sunken shipwrecks.

Some underwater robots are operated by remote-control from a ship on the surface. Others are more autonomous, and able to work on their own. Most are known as **ROVs** – remotely operated underwater vehicles. Radio signals cannot travel through water so ROVs have long cables or wires, known as tethers, to supply their electricity and carry information to and fro.

The cleverest ROVs are far more than simple remote-controlled gadgets. For example, they can sense sudden water currents that might tilt them over, and alter their propellers, rudders and fins so they stay upright and steady, all without human help.

A diver in a deep-sea pressure suit checks the ROV Achilles, which does not need any kind of suit. The Achilles series of deep-water robots can go down below 1000 metres.

Corals and canyons

ROVs carry out many tasks, especially surveys of ocean life and the sea bed. Scientists guide them through coral reefs, into underwater canyons and along the bottom. They watch the scene on the ROV's cameras as it records water temperature, pressure, currents and other measurements. This information helps us to understand how underwater earthquakes cause massive tsunami waves and how global warming is affecting the oceans.

Argo

In 1985 the wreck of the giant passenger ship Titanic, *which sank in 1912, was found about 3800 metres below the surface on the bed of the North Atlantic Ocean. Here the water's enormous pressure would kill a person instantly. The wreck was found by cameras on the sledge-like device Argo, towed just above the ocean floor by a massively long cable from a ship above. Was Argo a robot? Probably not. It could only take pictures and echo-soundings or sonar measurements. It could not move or make decisions on its own.*

Crew members prepare to lower Argo into the sea, on its way to detecting the wreck of the Titanic.

After the Titanic *was found on the sea bed, several ROVs and manned craft, such as Alvin, studied how it had sunk and what was left.*

Fight that fire!

Human firefighters brave perilous conditions such as blazing flames, burning heat, choking smoke, deadly fumes, collapsed buildings and the risk of explosion. More and more robots are helping to explore fire scenes, checking for hazards and making an area safe.

Robo-blog■

GETTING IN

'I'm part of the robot firefighting team. A great problem at our fire scenes is getting in, or access. Doors, roof beams and other objects fall and block the way. I have a very powerful arm and clip-on attachments such as grippers, snippers and even a circular saw. I can push, shove, lift, cut and slice a way through for my robot team-mates to enter. Then the human firefighters arrive – and they take all the credit. Unfair!'■

◄◄ *Firefighters wear clothing which protects them from heat and flames, a helmet to shield them from falling debris, and an oxygen tank and mask so they can breathe. Robots do not risk their lives – they are not alive.*

First at the scene

Firefighting robots come in various shapes and sizes, depending on the jobs they do. They are strong, tough and heat-resistant, especially to flames and falling items. Scout robots search and explore, usually on a long electrical cable or tether. Like SAR-bots, they are small and slim so they can fit through narrow gaps. Many have tracks or are multi-wheeled so they can climb stairs and trundle over rubble. Their cameras take pictures of the scene and send them back to display screens at the control base. They also have temperature sensors and some carry chemical sensors to detect dangerous fumes and gases.

Damping down

Bigger, stronger robots carry a water hose or foam sprayer to the best position for aiming at the fire. The hose trails along behind. Water and foam hoses are heavy to pull, and when they are turned they give a strong jerk, so they need to be held very firmly. Cameras on these robots allow their human controllers to see where to spray. Gradually the robots put out the flames and damp down very hot objects such as glowing metal and smouldering wood.

▶▶ *This red fire extinguisher can be aimed and squirted by its robot, which moves close to the flames on heatproof caterpillar tracks.*

The Hovereye mini-helicopter robot surveys a fire from above, giving its controller (on the right) a bird's-eye view. This helps the team to aim their hoses in the most effective way.

Robots at war

Few places are more dangerous than a war zone or battlefield. Army soldiers, air force pilots and navy sailors risk serious injury and death. Military robots are used for many different tasks to save lives and prevent suffering.

On the battlefield

Armies fight with tanks, armoured cars, missile-launching trucks and soldiers on foot. Robot versions of all these are being tested to see whether they can prevent soldiers dying or suffering serious injuries.

Big tanks are driven by people. Mini-tanks are well-protected robot versions that go ahead of troops to send back information about enemy forces.

This fighting robot has a gun fixing on top that can fire a variety of clip-on weapons, including bullets, rocket-propelled grenades and high-pressure gas jets.

Every few years, the US Defense Advanced Research Projects Agency (DARPA) holds its Grand Challenge in a remote area. Unmanned robotic vehicles have to find their way around a complicated route and carry out a series of tasks by themselves, with no human control. The Grand Challenge is partly fun, as well as helping to advance robot technology. It also shows how, one day, supplies might be carried around a war zone by robot trucks.

Could robot soldiers replace human ones? Any robot can suddenly go wrong. A rogue robot with a machine gun or grenade launcher might be as likely to fire at its own side as at the enemy.

Against the law

Designing robots to attack and kill people goes against the three laws of robotics. These are not real laws but imaginary rules made up by science-fiction writer Isaac Asimov in 1942. The first law says that a robot should not injure a human being or allow a human being to come to harm. Military chiefs would probably say that the laws are designed for peacetime. In wartime, anything goes – even killer-bots.

 Human pilots guide the Team Terrahawk robot vehicle on a test run before the DARPA Grand Challenge.

ROBO-FUTURE

Starship Troopers

The three Starship Troopers movies (1997, 2004, 2008) feature massive battles between humans and aliens, including spider-like Bugs. Parts of the story were based on a 1959 book of the same name by Robert Heinlein. In the book, the soldiers wear powered armour suits which copy their movements and make them much bigger, stronger and more dangerous. Also in this future time, medical advances heal the human troopers' wounds very quickly – almost like fitting a new part to a robot.

Eye in the sky

In future wars there may be many kinds of military robots on the battlefield – and above it too. One of the best ways to spy on an enemy is from the sky. Already there are many types of robot aircraft called **drones** which fly over enemy regions or areas where there are suspicious activities. Their job is to sneak in, spy by taking photographs and escape as quickly as possible.

Under the radar

Drones are known as UAVs or unmanned aerial vehicles – they have no pilots or crew. Usually they fly very low, where they cannot be detected by the other side's **radar**. They take photographs and send these back to base in the form of radio signals. The photographs show information such as the number of tanks at an army base or aircraft at an air centre.

Jamming signals

Some drones are mainly remote-controlled by radio signals from their base. Their human masters tell them where to fly and when to take pictures. But the enemy may detect the control signals to the drone or the photograph signals it sends back. The enemy could then block or jam these radio signals, or send more powerful signals to take over the drone and make it crash or fly to their own base.

The CPX4 drone is a quadrocopter, with four separate whirling rotors to hover and move through the air. It can stay up for 30 minutes and take hundreds of pictures with its central camera.

◄◄ *Infrared or heat-sensitive images, such as this picture of an air base, can be taken at night, when it's very difficult to detect the quiet drone in the darkness.*

Radio silence

Clever drones need fewer instructions. Their computers, **satnavs** and **GPS** equipment have enough information to decide where to go and what to photograph. The information is stored on board until the drone returns to base. So the drone can complete its mission without receiving or sending radio signals – known as radio silence. The silence makes it more difficult for the enemy to detect, as does the drone's small size and quietness.

▼ *The 8.22-metre-long Predator spyplane is armed with a Hellfire missile under its right wing. The ball-shaped camera under the nose swivels around to point at any angle.*

ROBOT SUPERSTAR

Warrior and Predator

The MQ-1C Sky Warrior first flew in 2008. It will replace the MQ-1 Predator, which has spied on many regions. Warrior is eight metres long, with wings that measure 17 metres across. That's big enough to carry a pilot, but Warrior doesn't need one. It flies at almost 250 kilometres per hour and can take thousands of photographs – and even shoot Hellfire or Stinger missiles.

97-3034

Robo navy

Robotic ships and submarines carry out many military tasks. One is **reconnaissance** – patrolling an area to look, listen and sense anything strange or unusual. Like reconnaissance aircraft, these unmanned ships find their way using satellite navigation. Some of them have guns or even torpedoes (underwater missiles) so they can fire back if attacked.

Robo-patrols

The robot reconnaissance boat Spartan Scout was designed for the US Navy. Dozens are now used by other countries too for various purposes. Spartan Scout can patrol a harbour or coastline to look for smugglers trying to bring cargo into a country illegally, to check for fishing boats in places where fish are protected, and to find terrorists who might be planning an attack.

▼ *AMN 1, standing for Autonomous Maritime Navigation, is a US Navy test craft. Here it speeds through its trial runs, controlling itself, although a boat pilot and an engineer take a ride just in case things go wrong.*

Dangers at sea

Spartan Scout is almost seven metres long and weighs two tonnes. It records what happens using daylight and night-time cameras, a microphone, radar and other sensors. It detects other boats, explosive mines, submarines and other dangers. After being programmed by its human masters, this robo-boat work can on its own using satnav for up to 48 hours. Or it can be operated by remote control from a ship.

Ahoy there!

If Spartan Scout finds a suspicious boat, the controllers can watch the scene through its cameras. They can also speak to the boat's crew using a loudspeaker on Spartan Scout, and hear what the crew say through its microphones. If someone shoots, the robot boat can fire back using its powerful machine gun.

Ordinary satellite navigation, as used in cars, is not as accurate as the military version, which has special radio code signals to pinpoint a location to within a metre or two.

Big waves and jagged rocks are serious dangers at sea, but it's better to lose a robot than risk human lives.

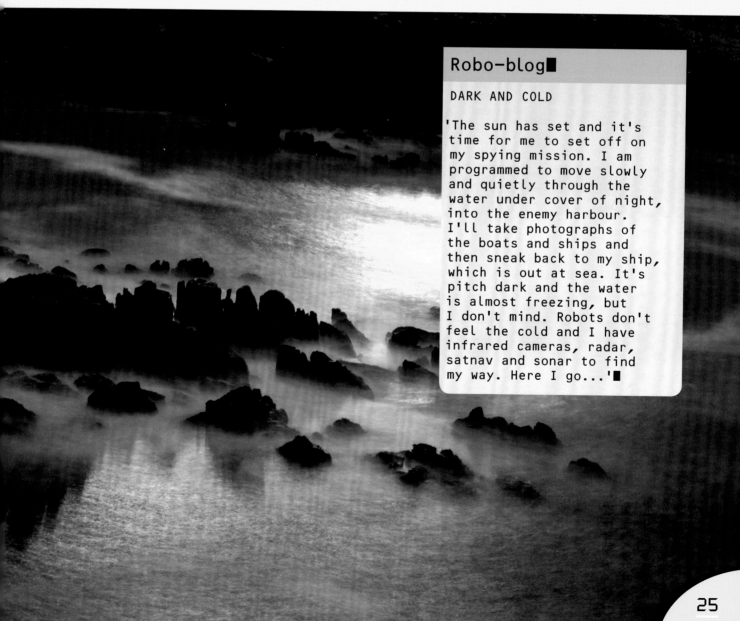

Robo-blog ■

DARK AND COLD

'The sun has set and it's time for me to set off on my spying mission. I am programmed to move slowly and quietly through the water under cover of night, into the enemy harbour. I'll take photographs of the boats and ships and then sneak back to my ship, which is out at sea. It's pitch dark and the water is almost freezing, but I don't mind. Robots don't feel the cold and I have infrared cameras, radar, satnav and sonar to find my way. Here I go...'■

Bomb disposal

Few things are as dangerous as an unexploded bomb. Old wartime bombs, modern terrorist bombs, forgotten landmines and **IEDs** (improvized explosive devices) cause tragedies daily around the world. For many years robots have helped to prevent these disasters and save people from horrific injuries and even death.

Bomb-disposal robot Remotec HD-1 prepares to pick up a dangerous object. It has a colour camera so its operator can see the scene, all-terrain caterpillar tracks and a telescopic arm with a grabbing pincer.

Mechanical fingers

Bomb disposal experts are trained to examine an explosive device, disarm or **defuse** it so it cannot go off, take it apart carefully, and get rid of the materials safely. Where possible, they send a robot to approach the device. This has various cameras and microphones, and manipulator arms fitted with grabs, cutters and similar tools. With the help of its operator, the robo-disposer stays calm and cool under pressure.

Tricks and traps

Using a robot, bomb disposal experts can study a device, hear noises such as a ticking timer, and poke or move parts, all from a safe distance. Bomb-makers often build tricks and traps into their devices, such as vibration sensors that can feel a trembling hand, or that make the bomb explode if it is moved. So bomb-bots must be precise and accurate, engineered to very high standards, in case a slight jolt sets off a vibration sensor.

▼ In this real-life scene an army bomb disposal robot moves cautiously towards a possible terrorist device – to find out that it's a trick or hoax, and the 'bomb' is false.

Some bomb disposal robots can open a car door, look inside, check a suspect device, lift it out carefully and carry it away to a safer place, ready to be exploded. Despite the combined skills of an expert human operator and a robot, accidents do happen. Some robots are blown to pieces. But that's a tiny price to pay for saving a human life.

◀◀ A bomb has just exploded inside a car. The bomb-disposal robot investigating the car was also damaged, but later repaired.

War and peace

Around the world, people continue to face hazards, such as natural disasters, accidents and wars. Designers and engineers are building improved robots that are stronger, smarter and more skilled and these can prevent more people being injured or killed in the future.

Various versions of the PackBot series of robots are designed to 'sniff' the air for traces of explosives, detect different rays and waves, listen for suspicious noises, or carry out a suicide mission by setting off a bomb.

Smart wheels

Robots sometimes find themselves in small places where it is difficult to move around. One solution is to fit them with special wheels. These are ball-shaped and have several small rollers or discs spread around the surface. By varying the speed and direction of the whole wheel and its rollers or discs, the robot can move forwards, backwards, sideways and even spin around on the spot. Bomb disposal robots have these wheels, as well as robots that undertake more light-hearted activities, such as playing sports and dancing.

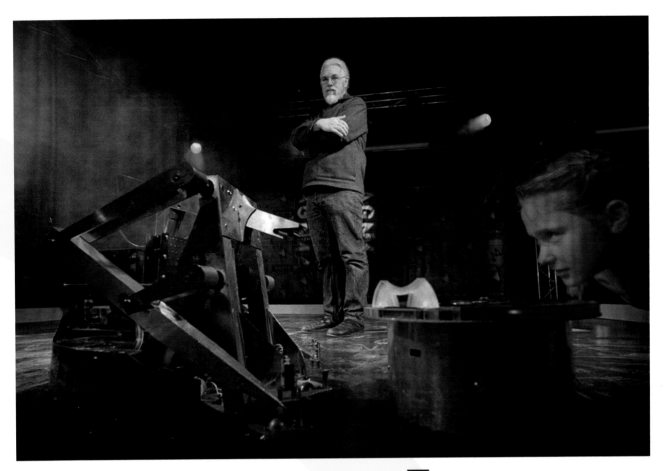

Robots on the road

Robot Wars is not a real battle but a TV series that travels around the country. The robots, their equipment and their human operators turn up at a sports hall, stadium or similar venue and get ready. People come to the live event to watch the action, support their favourites and cheer the winners. It's fun – and useful. Inventors and engineers at these events can come up with new ideas that can be adapted for robots with real work to do, such as those in factories or doing dirty, dangerous work.

 The Robot Wars *show pits various kinds of fun-fighting robots against each other, and also encourages progress in robot design and technology.*

Rollers called omni wheels make robots much more manoeuvrable or agile and able to get out of tight spots.

ROBO-FUTURE

Octo-bot

Like a combination of octopus and crab, Octo-bot is a test version, or prototype, of a new kind of undersea robot. It is designed to go into deep, dark water, move around using its four claw-like grabbers, and find its way by touch alone. Its outer surface is covered with tiny strip-shaped touch sensors, called electronic strain gauges, each about half as wide as a human hair. The robot can detect the slightest touch as it feels its way along and even react to water currents. Future versions may help to repair oil rigs and undersea pipelines or take samples of rocks and mud from the ocean floor.

Glossary of robo-terms

ammonia
A dangerous chemical. In the form of a gas, ammonia can damage our bodies or even kill us, by harming our lungs.

arc
A continuous hot, bright spark produced by a very powerful electric current.

autonomous
A machine or device that mostly controls itself and works on its own, without human control, as most robots do.

avalanche
A sliding mass of snow and ice that rolls or tumbles down a slope with unstoppable force.

carbon monoxide
A dangerous gas usually produced by burning. Carbon monoxide can damage our bodies. It can even kill people by suffocation (stopping them breathing).

chlorine
A dangerous chemical. In the form of a gas, chlorine can damage our bodies, or even kill us, by harming our lungs and airways.

climate change
Changes in day-to-day weather and long term climate, mainly caused by global warming (see right).

crevasse
A deep slit or crack in snow or ice.

cryo-resistant material
A substance that is not damaged by extremely low temperatures, for example, below –100° Celsius.

defuse
To make safe a bomb or similar device, so it cannot explode.

drive units
Devices that make a robot or similar machine move along. These are usually electric motors.

drone
The general name for an unmanned vehicle or robot, especially a flying one. They mainly control themselves or can be operated by humans by remote control.

electrical-magnetic waves
Waves of combined electrical and magnetic energy, including radio waves, microwaves, light rays and X-rays.

global warming
The gradual heating up of the Earth as a result of increasing amounts of some gases in the atmosphere, especially the carbon dioxide produced when we burn fossil fuels and other fuels.

GPS
Stands for Global Positioning System – more than 20 satellites that travel around the Earth and send out radio signals. These are detected by a GPS receiver to show the receiver's position and help to find the way or navigate. Often called satnav.

hazardous
Possibly dangerous or harmful.

heavy metal
A metal which is very heavy or weighty, such as lead or uranium.

IED
Stands for improvized explosive device. This is a bomb made from everyday materials, rather than one made by military experts.

infrared
Light with waves slightly longer than red light waves. Our eyes cannot see infrared waves, but some animals' eyes can. Infrared rays carry heat.

manipulators
Devices that handle or hold something carefully, and move it or its parts precisely.

oil refineries
Huge industrial areas where crude oil, or petroleum, is turned into hundreds of useful products, from petrol and other fuels, to paints and varnishes.

radar
Sending out radio signals and detecting them when they bounce off an object. They show the size, shape and distance of the object.

radioactive
Sending out harmful but invisible rays and tiny particles called radiation, that can damage living things, including the human body.

reconnaissance
Looking around an area, perhaps in secret, to gather information.

ROV
Stands for remotely operated vehicle. ROVs are usually underwater craft controlled by a person, or craft which are robotic and mainly able to control themselves.

satnav
Short for satellite navigation, which is finding the way using a GPS receiver that detects radio signals from satellites going around the Earth.

sensors
Devices that detect and measure something, such as a camera which measures light, a microphone which measures sound, or a magnetometer which measures magnetic forces.

thermo-resistant material
A substance that is not damaged by extremely high temperatures, for example, temperatures above 100° Celsius (the temperature at which water boils).

toxic
Poisonous or harmful in some way – often describes dangerous chemicals.

tsunami
A huge wave or series of waves set off by an undersea earthquake or volcanic eruption. The wave crashes on to the shore and causes immense damage.

uranium
A type of metal that is very hard and heavy, and can be radioactive in some forms.

welding rod
A long, stick-like metal rod used to weld or join metal parts. The welding rod is heated and melts into the narrow gap between the metal parts.

Further reading

Robots by Clive Gifford (Carlton Books 2008)

Building Robots with LEGO Mindstorms NXT by Mario Ferrari (Syngress 2007)

Robot by Roger Bridgman (DK Eyewitness Books 2004)

Learn About Robotics (Sci Faxes) by De-Ann Black (Top That! 2005)

Robots and Robotics series: How Robots Work and other titles Tony Hyland (Macmillan Library, Nelson Thornes 2008)

Ultimate Robot by Robert Malone (Dorling Kindersley 2004)

Websites

Robot World News
This site covers the top news stories on robotics, artificial intelligence and related areas, but it also has more fun information on robots such as toys.
http://www.robotworldnews.com/robots4u.html

Robot video clips
Video clips of all kinds of robots in action.
http://www.robotclips.com/

Robot Wars
In the popular *Robot Wars* competitions, teams strive to improve robots of all kinds, not just for battle – see especially the SAFETY page.
http://www.ukrobotwars.com/mains.htm

Index